ON TIME

ON TIME

Poems

DONALD MACKAY

MARISCAT
PRESS 2012

ISBN 978 0 946588 62 6

Acknowledgements

'Kirk of Bruan' was first published in *The Dark Horse*
24; 'Flambeaux' was joint winner of the Neil Gunn
Prize, 2011; 'Sea-Ware' was featured in the exhibition
'A Sense of Place: New Jewellery from Northern Lands'
at the National Museum of Scotland, Summer 2012.

Designed and typeset by Gerry Cambridge
gerry.cambridge@btinternet.com
Set in Plantin MT and Castellar

Printed by Clydeside Press, 37 High Street,
Glasgow G1 1LX
clydesidepress@btconnect.com

Published by Mariscat Press, 10 Bell Place,
Edinburgh EH3 5HT
www.mariscatpress.co.uk
hamish.whyte@btinternet.com

CONTENTS

On Time / 7

Aberdeen Angus / 8

Kirk of Bruan / 9

Tirana-Inverness-Tirana / 10

The Johnson Collection / 11

A Vacancy / 12

Tom-All-Alone's / 13

Flambeaux / 14

A Covenant / 15

At Hugh Mackay's, Scourie / 16

Raring to Go / 17

The Boundary / 18

Together / 19

Time No More / 20

Mayflies / 21

Cremation / 22

Earth's Leavings / 23

Sea-Ware / 24

Worked / 25

Terry's / 26

String Quartet / 27

A Chinese Colander / 28

Storage / 29

A Canon / 30

A Player / 31

For Mum and Dad

ON TIME

Arriving Glasgow half an hour before
tomorrow had begun,
The Herald (but today's *Le Figaro*)
The Daily Record and *The Scottish Sun*

I found it odd
that I could know what they would say,
like God,
tomorrow, while it was still today

the clocks had struck, my train was in
the Edinburgh 12.04,
last night's last-train party-goers wishing
already it was still the day before.

ABERDEEN ANGUS

A stolid herd, solidly black, heavily-thighed,
scattered across the field
spend every evening fully-occupied
with grass, stuffing the manifold

which is the process of their elongated gut,
their thick jaw-muscles chewing
and chewing and chewing on the cud.
Over the road are fat black bales, eschewing

head or tail but likewise filled
inside their thinnish skin of polythene
with bundled hay, the contents of a field

its cellulose and protein
for the season's turn, when summer's failed
and fat black bales turn into cows, repeating.

KIRK OF BRUAN

I was once told of a man
who kept his beasts in the Kirk of Bruan,
after the Free Church had left, of course.

Went clean skite
the cattle, bawling and slobbering all night;
Mad-Cow Disease, probably

though many took the view
that he'd committed a terrible profanity
by housing them alongside God.

For myself, I'd prefer a decent cow
to most Christians;
but then, I'm not God.

TIRANA-INVERNESS-TIRANA

An old and oddly-swaddled couple waddled-on,
here from Albania maybe or Kazakhstan
and talking loudly in a *language*
as if Scotrail, Empire narrow-gauge
Kingdom Brunel had never been,
as if this was Albania, Uzbekistan or Spain
and she'd a wicker basket, clucking chicken
on a slatted train from local town to kitchen.

Trains are the *lingua-franca* of a world
that's poor and speaks only a little English,
Portuguese perhaps or Quechua, Italian
Scots or Cantonese; in which you learn,
from childhoods spent on trains, how to unfold
your own small world. I saw her carrier release
tomatoes in a handkerchief with eggs, them leaning
together on their table over it, half-silent.

THE JOHNSTON COLLECTION*

Seeing Bridge Street the way it was before;
there's the Caledonian Hotel
gone, the Universal Outfitters, B. Forbes
also gone, the lampost halt

of loiterers in cloth caps posed, moved-on.
Only the stillness of the attic windows
where a too soft curtain, washed too often
so that it undoes

across the middle; this you may find
in the windows of the wrong street any day,
the unrefined
way of making-do with less. Some things stay.

*A collection of 19th to mid 20th century photographs of the town
by a firm of Wick photographers.

A VACANCY

The herringers most weekdays sit
under the iron Market,
nothing caught.
You catch the handrolled cigarette

around the corner, recreate
three men or four and are correct,
caught in the act
of nothing, who now are the fleet

as harbour walls vacate
the yawls whose berths collect
an emptiness. Boats they'll locate
as still and open waters indicate.

TOM-ALL-ALONE'S

Under an arch and down the court, a door;
behind a mist of dust, a light
dim in one window
where it must always be too late

even at noon. A badly-written sign
DONT BREAK IN SOMEBODY LIVES HERE
pinned on the door, by no one
never a sign of him or her

merely a low bulb fitfully
inside a tenement
where, as the records show, nobody's lived
only some poor lost soul, condemned.

FLAMBEAUX

On the Selembao stalls, cloth wicked in palm oil
made a carnival of fire: planks, two oil drums
on them *chikwangu*, smokefish, tinned sardines
avocados, mangos, bananas,
bread which had been fresh that morning

whatever anyone could buy and sell, was fine
on such a night after a storm, in such a light.
People grew happy, for rain had relaxed the air
and a flicker of flames shone our skin like oil
making us all, in that most primitive of lights,

singularly beautiful.
How? Total strangers would press my hands
as if we were all *muisi-Kongo* for tonight
and the thin high music from the *boites de nuit*
shook everybody's hips,

on every hand, *'Kiambote'*. Not at all romantic,
only to me in the sharp lack of an electric light.
It was simply the way things are
when people, even with a *mundele*
in their middle, practically become themselves.

chikwangu: cassava puddings;
muisi-Kongo: Bakongo;
boites de nuit: brothels;
Kiambote: ki-Kongo greeting;
mundele: European

A COVENANT

Uncle Cameron, the last man in his tenement
visited on Christmas Day;
getting up meant
climbing by still-lit gaslight all the way

and there he was, Cameronian
dark front door, flaking blue walls, or green
one table, two chairs. There were no
carpets, boards scrubbed clean, very clean

blue walls, blue sky beyond the windows
in the prophetic echo of his tenement
high over Port Dundas;
as if we had slipped inside the other Testament.

AT HUGH MACKAY'S, SCOURIE

For Chester Kelly

Nettles were standing sodden nearly five foot tall
wrapping the house
within their green electric wall.
It was still raining too hard, but I recall it as

a fishing day. The masonry
as if it had been weighted underwater
stood so rimmed around with blazoned greenery
it was at first too dim to see. A platter

shone in the firelight, an enormous salmon
filling the chatter full of fishermen because,
though boys or lesser men,
we grew to heroes with the shadows of the house.

RARING TO GO

For A.F.

as if a bike had stuck inside her driving
her full-throttle say a Honda
two-stroke in her head
had kept revving on and on and
on since she had suddenly seen red
racing with time but never yet arriving

she was dying someone said
and all that evening
after tea-time
we heard nothing but her heaving
heavy death as every breath kept rhythm
with her dynamo—I wished her dead

or nearly so she'd stop
as I lay wakeful hearing her in bed
that roar that wild accelerating roar
inside my head
until I woke at four
and didn't hear her leave as she sped off

THE BOUNDARY

A dyke run through the middle of nowhere
and in it a gate,
nothing to indicate
which side of nowhere we are on

heather, tussocky grass and spaghnum
bogland, with this intricate
wrought-iron gate
standing wide-openly, telling us, 'Come!'

The wall is fallen but this after all is a gate
and so we, two
by two, like sheep into

a pasture, pass on through
so that we'll get
somewhere imagined, knowing it isn't true.

TOGETHER

Picking on either side of gooseberries
where spines of several centimetres
on a line of bushes separate
as surely as a line of scimitars

a rosy wall that cuts the prince
off from the princess.
Such a sharpness
in our conversation represents

the edge we'll never lack
that distance
where a body easily may look
yet hardly reach; which is the actual dance.

TIME NO MORE

It always is the moment after, time has passed
but only just. As when you've just let-
go of her, too close for it to last
and she's continued cooking, so it's now too late

or that time he left for good, just two hours after
you on the street
were unaccountably afraid
to say hello, by being driven straight

into another—
time which each day has passed you
inexorably, seems somehow thinner,

almost as if you'd reach back into then for her
or him; as if at-root
you knew, time unaccounted-for cannot be true.

MAYFLIES

Let those whose bodies, all uneven, hang
held in the sun's straight rays,
become the measure of this evening.
On their delight the sunlight concentrates—

more and more rise, far as the eye can see,
so tiny yet electrical with light.
No space for flesh in such transparency
only for sun, shifting as it grows late

to yellow
slowly turning into gold.
Then, as it starts to sink below,
they faint and vanish. All at once, it's cold.

CREMATION

That last day, I couldn't see you for the smoke
drifting over Erskine.
All that you'd left of clothes, skin,
flesh, you hurried off and never spoke

then you were gone, more or less
vanished and dispersed. An east wind blowing
brought you high over Bowling
Port Glasgow, Dumbarton, other places

further west. One lucky man began bearing
traces of you
that sifted down, as the air carrying

your effortless burden, manfully flew
on out to sea; how bright the Clyde, how blue
the sea and sky, that day all you were wearing.

EARTH'S LEAVINGS

'...sur terre ont paru les feuilles'
—Rimbaud, *Les Fêtes de la Faim*

Red rocks that snap-off, the leaves that are leaving
at the crack of the sea or the wind's whip
into a nakedness numb beyond all feeling

see the tree high on a headland has become a ship
leaving port in a storm,
a rowan nearly-unrigged that will soon slip

with its rocky cargo into the stream
of an outgoing tide,
putting-out without sail or mast, bow or stern

into its growl as it's emptied,
sometime back on its return
with the pillars of stone that the sea has stumped

whose detritus, frozen leaves forever on the turn
are as livid a russet or red as fragments of the living
that are dying, the fossils of an everlasting autumn.

SEA-WARE

Great gales that flew here from north of Svalbard
have felled the lost forest of the sea,
whose olive sluice and sway
we first see as the swell lifts it on-board

root and branch, onto our rocky shore.
Here are stems which rose straight into the blue
while, far below,
shifting across the forest floor

stars and radiant urchins glimmered in the dark.
Work to align yourself
with what the sea has logged, as it falls

broken wrack, off every wave and onto our deck,
living fossils
from that bottom shelf, where our bodies still rock.

WORKED

Stones which are worthless, taking form
from common salts of silica
a little random manganese or iron
maybe mercury and mud, polished to silk

again and again inside my idle hand,
a rub of body-oil
and trouser-leg, at my command
or rather through my toil

turn into colour, faceted light and depth
containing, see
in that patina, a path
through many chances of millenia, to me.

TERRY'S

he'd thought he knew how dark can be
blacker than a blackout blind
than the land
on the shore of that dark sea

as black as black can be
until she takes his hand
and out they step into a darker land
where nothing can be told by

staring-at and yet he's happy
for she has his hand
they walk a little then they stand

a snap
of chocolate and
he can taste how sweet the dark can be

STRING QUARTET

Wind, which in itself is only space, is silent
till it harps each string
of grass in passing
or of barley, blowing them through aslant

each reed, each wind-blown instrument
only a thing of wind,
the one note rushing-together to one end
driven like souls in torment

who are rooted in a race that never ends
or even leaves
though yet again, and yet again, it flees

both to and from me, as the wind unwinds
embroiders round me, all-around my face,
catches within a tapestry, hare and hounds.

A CHINESE COLANDER

After a bit the lengthy years get measured out
in pets,
the first year of the dog
the month of the gerbils

onward through rabbits, stick insects, cats
until we arrive at the present
year of the triops (don't ask),
their little lives and bigger deaths
which lack any permanent memorial

only the occasional photograph
they happened to step-into,
stones discovered in weeds I'll leave to cover
spots where I cannot dig

also their scale. It was the size of your hand,
a gerbil,
can you feel it still, the size of your hand
the size of a gerbil?
Be careful now. My God! Don't drop it or you'll

STORAGE

The hardest I've ever done was the store,
an archeology of sixteen years
as I dug through layers with no logic,
only a history of sorts, so dense it hurt

being slapped about by little garments
gloves that no longer fitted,
the bottoms of a swimsuit she wore
in Harare. And right down at the bottom

trousers from the three-piece I'd bought
in Mothercare, blue for the boy
she was not but, stunned by its littleness
I never thought. She'd maybe wear it now

as a two-fingered glove. Though she'd not,
of no interest to her. Nor I,
love has no interest in another
but pays without consideration. Is hardest.

A CANON

I was alone, more stretched than I could say.
I heard the wind, I heard the willow sway
against the window pane. No one would stay
because of me, and so the house lay

empty around me all-alone. I heard myself
twist with the wind, unable to resolve
myself to any end, each thought of love
equally hate. In-between them I'd revolve

like wind catching the corners of the house,
it out and me within, as if I was
wind's vicious complement. And then a pause;
that sense of sense, the silence of the wise.

A PLAYER

The lady who is carrying her cello
on-board the train,
that instrument
now seated opposite

looks like her double and a friend,
almost a perfect fit.
Being alone, don't think her lonely
just because she's plain

she's very self-contained,
her ticket's a return
to playing, not a quick hello-
goodbye but love. See how they sit.